Table of Contents

Some of the most popular *Roblox* games ask players to team up and battle against computer-controlled enemies.

Unlimited Adventure

Are you a *Roblox* fan? More than 100 million people per month log on to *Roblox* to play games. These games are created by other *Roblox* users. There are millions of them to choose from. Some of these games allow players to compete against each other. Others encourage players to join forces and **cooperate** to win.

Huge crowds of players can gather in the most popular *Roblox* games.

Sharing the Fun

Playing with other people is a big part of the fun in *Roblox*. But remember that most of the people you meet in *Roblox* are **strangers**. You need to be very careful anytime you deal with strangers online. Most of the people you'll meet will probably be *Roblox* fans just like you. But you can never know for sure.

Get Permission

Always ask a parent or other trusted adult before you sign up for a new online game. It is easier to stay safe online if someone knows which games you play.

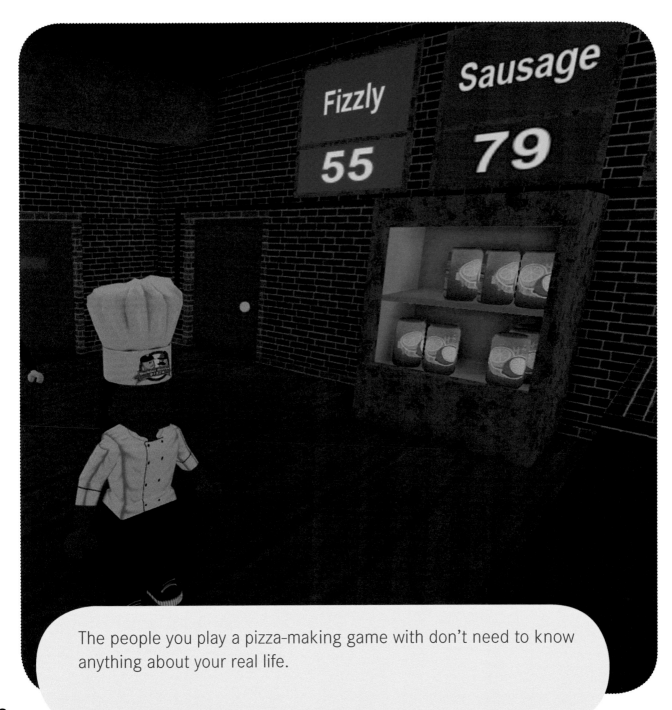

The people you play a pizza-making game with don't need to know anything about your real life.

Personal Information

The main key to staying safe online is keeping your personal information secret. What is personal information? It is anything that could help strangers figure out your **identity** or location. Your real name is one example of personal information. So is your address. Even the names of your school and hometown count as personal information.

CherryLakePub

Friends | Followers | Following
0 | 0 | 0

About   Creations

About

Re

Currently Wearing

3D

● ○

Player Badges

S

First Joi

Every *Roblox* player has a profile page like this one. Don't put any personal information here.

Choosing a Username

The first step to staying safe on *Roblox* is to choose the right username. Don't use your real name. In fact, don't use any personal information at all. Try to make up a completely unique name that has nothing to do with your real life. This can be a lot of fun! Be creative. Don't be afraid to go with something that sounds funny or strange.

Built-in Protection

Roblox has many built-in features to protect its players from dangerous people online. For example, the game does not allow certain words to be used in usernames or chats.

The chat window is in the top left part of the screen. Sometimes, messages will also appear above your character's head when you type them.

Chatting Safely

Many *Roblox* games have a chat window. Here, players can type messages to each other as they play. This is a good way to plan and use teamwork. But be careful what you say. Try to talk only about the game. You don't have to answer if someone asks you a question about yourself. Just ignore them or change the subject.

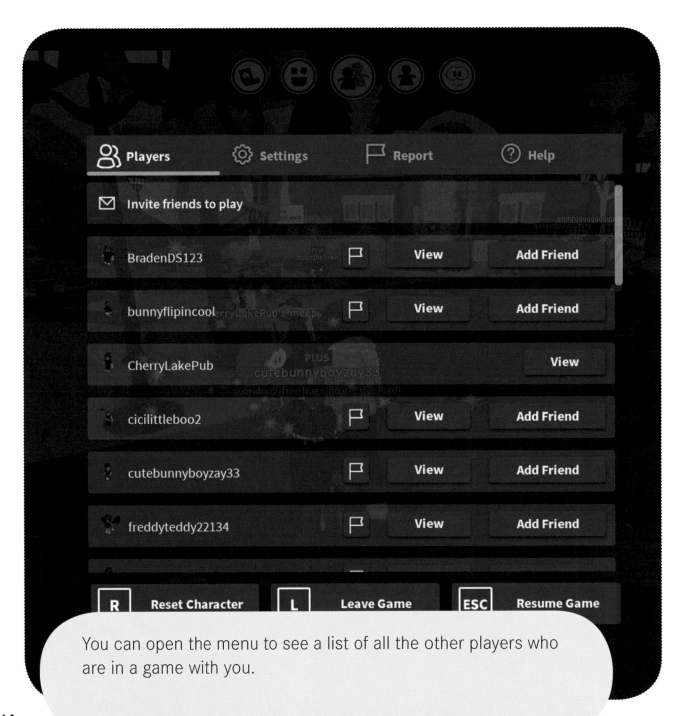

Players Settings Report Help

Invite friends to play

BradenDS123 | View | Add Friend

bunnyflipincool | View | Add Friend

CherryLakePub | View

cicilittleboo2 | View | Add Friend

cutebunnyboyzay33 | View | Add Friend

freddyteddy22134 | View | Add Friend

R Reset Character   L Leave Game   ESC Resume Game

You can open the menu to see a list of all the other players who are in a game with you.

14

Making New Friends

You might have a really good time playing with certain people you meet on *Roblox*. Maybe you'd like to add them to your in-game friends list. Then you can play together again later on. This is OK! Just remember that these people are still strangers. Don't share personal information.

Keep It Online

Don't ever agree to meet up with an online friend in person. Tell a trusted adult right away if someone online asks you to meet them offline.

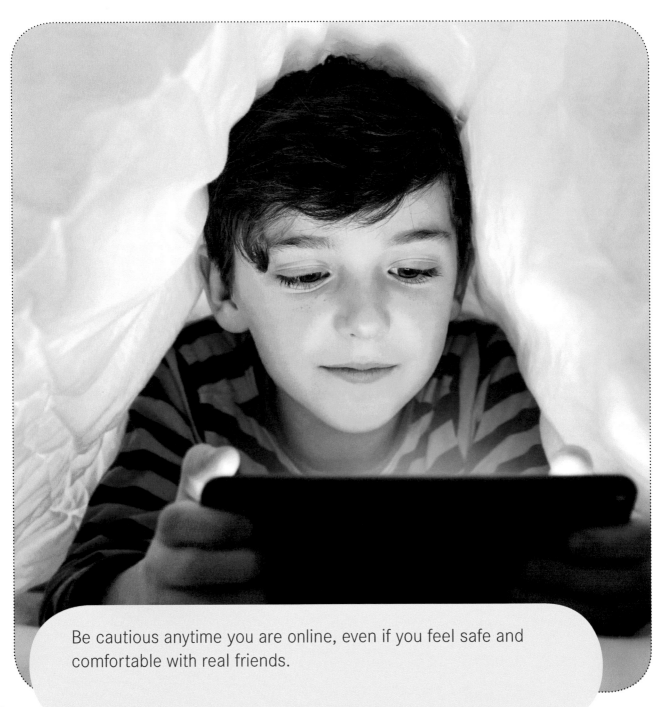

Be cautious anytime you are online, even if you feel safe and comfortable with real friends.

Going Online with Offline Friends

You might sometimes play *Roblox* with friends you know in real life. But don't let your guard down completely. Don't discuss real-life things with your friends in public chat windows. Other players will be able to see it. There is also a private chat window you can use. Only your friends can see that one. Even in private chat, don't type anything you don't want others to see. Your friend could share it by mistake.

Try asking your parents to play *Roblox* with you. They might like to see how much fun it can be!

What to Do When You Feel Unsafe

Someone you're playing with online could say or do something that makes you feel uncomfortable. If something seems wrong, don't wait. Leave the game right away. Then tell an adult you can trust. Be honest about what happened. Let an adult decide if it was OK or not.

There's no time to chat or reveal personal information when you're playing a fast-paced game of soccer!

Don't Be Afraid

Hearing about dangerous strangers online might make *Roblox* sound scary. But don't worry. Everything will be fine as long as you follow online safety rules. *Roblox* is a lot of fun to play. Relax and have a good time online with your friends. Remember that most of the players you meet are kids just like you. They are probably trying to stay safe online, too!

Glossary

cooperate (koh-AHP-ur-ate) work together

identity (eye-DEN-tih-tee) who you are

strangers (STRAYN-jurz) someone you don't know
or have never met in real life

Find Out More

Books

Cunningham, Kevin. *Video Game Designer*. Ann Arbor, MI: Cherry Lake Publishing, 2016.

Powell, Marie. *Asking Questions About Video Games*. Ann Arbor, MI: Cherry Lake Publishing, 2016.

Web Sites
Roblox
www.roblox.com
Sign up for a *Roblox* account, download the game, and start playing.

Roblox Support
https://en.help.roblox.com/hc/en-us
Find answers to common questions about *Roblox* and check out some guides to getting started.

Index

About the Author

Josh Gregory is the author of more than 150 books for kids. He has written about everything from animals to technology to history. A graduate of the University of Missouri–Columbia, he currently lives in Chicago, Illinois.